We dedicate this workbook to all the
families healing their money wounds and
working toward building generational wealth.

Parents,
This workbook includes coloring pages that not only
introduces children to the stock market, but provides a
fun tool for an educational conversation about investing.
From penmanship activities that will help develop their
writing skills to revisiting the alphabet with the help of stock
market vocabulary and illustrations, each page is a
combination of fun and education.

When going through the alphabet, we recommend
you teach the letters' sounds, not the actual
letter as practicing this will help children learn
to blend the letters, allowing for a smooth transition
into learning how to read. Towards the end
of the book, we introduce numbers through
counting, tracing and fun graphics.

This book was inspired by my mother,
Linda Garcia and her beginner stock market course;
Wealth Rules Everything Around Me.

XO
Elizabeth Ruiz

This Book Belongs To:

_____

- -

_____

The Fearless Girl

The fearless girl is a bronze sculpture by Kristen Visbal, commissioned by State Street Global Advisors located across from the New York Stock Exchange. She promotes female empowerment and represents gender diversity.

The market is your teacher.

Piggy Bank

What will you invest in?

Bull

Bear

Bullish Stock

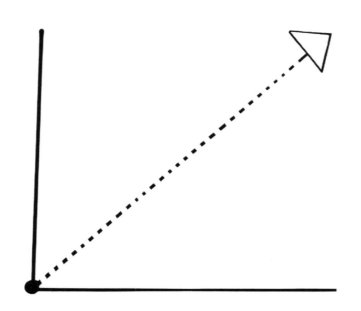

Bearish Stock

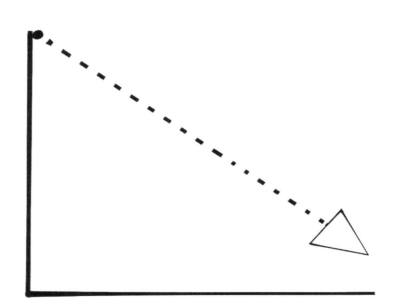

Trace the lines on the charts.

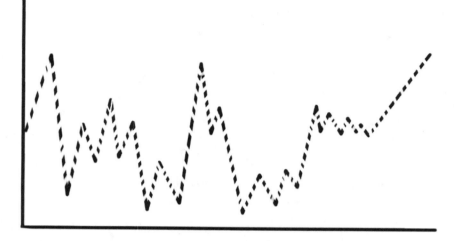

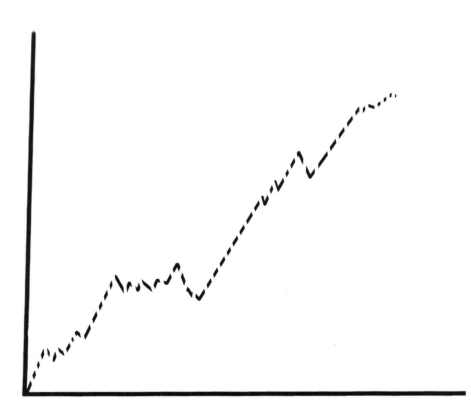

Charts are always moving.

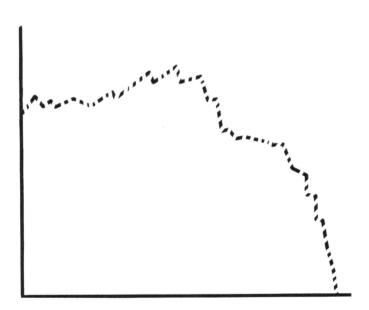

a

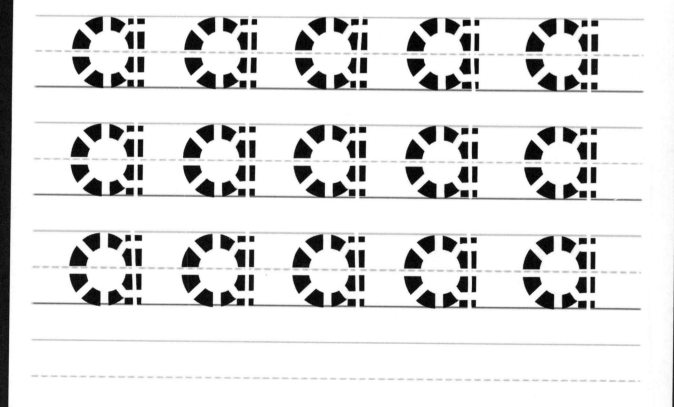

assets

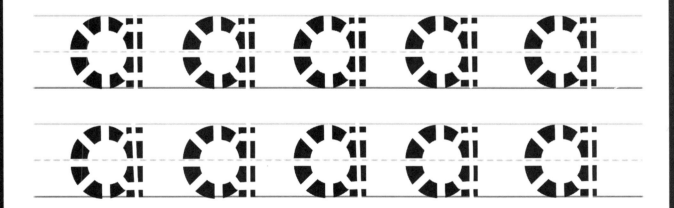

b

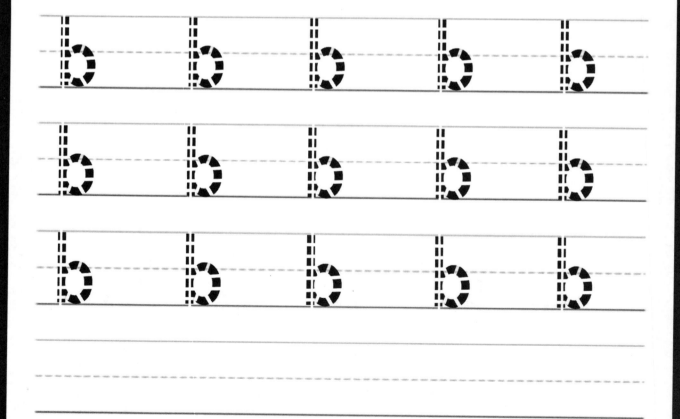

bank

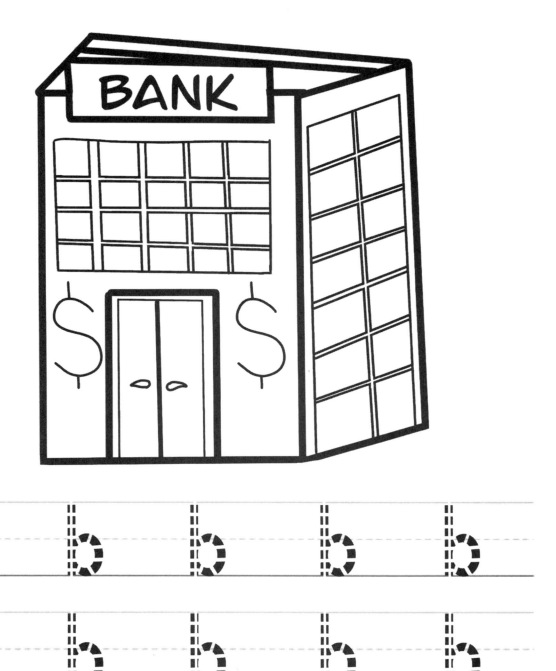

C

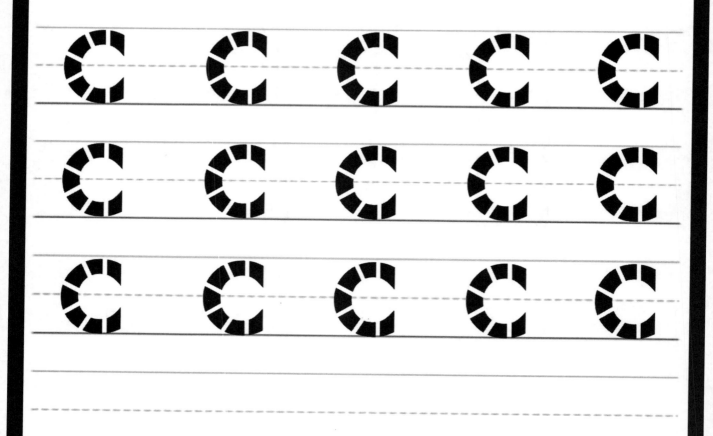

capital

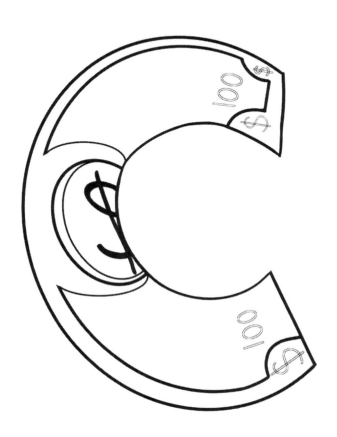

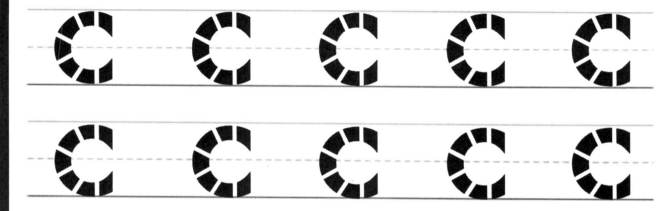

d

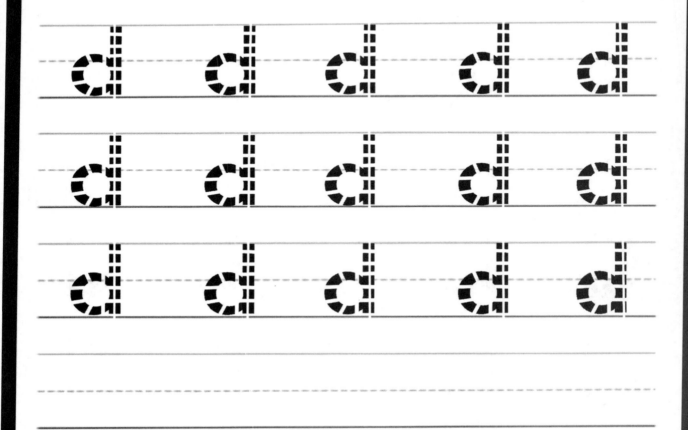

debt

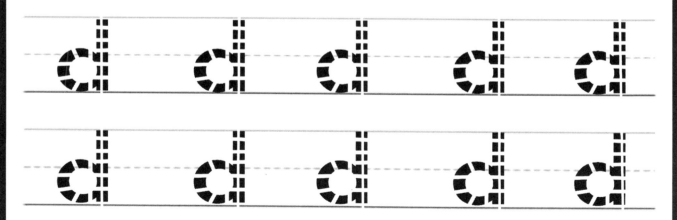

e

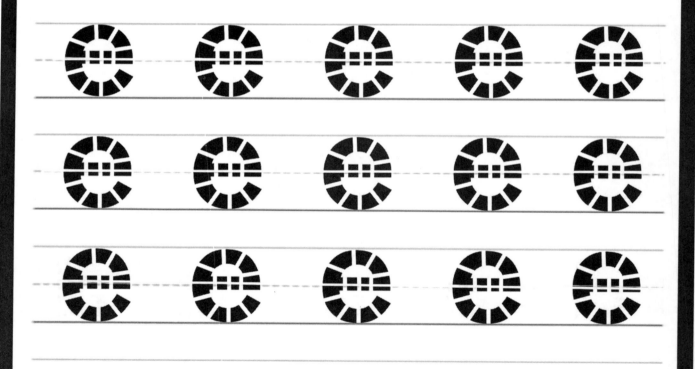

exchange

f

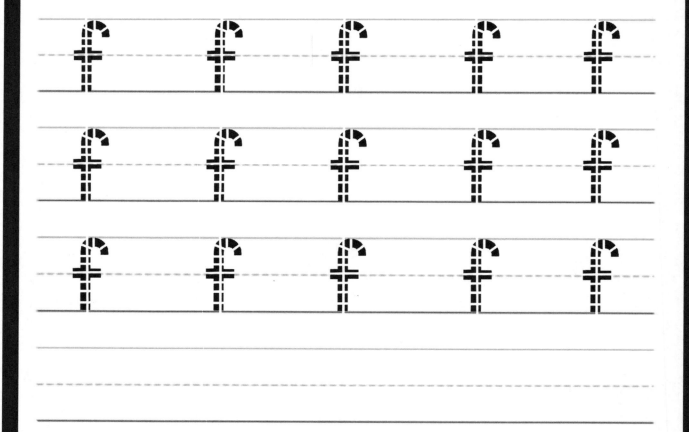

future

f f f f f

f f f f f

g

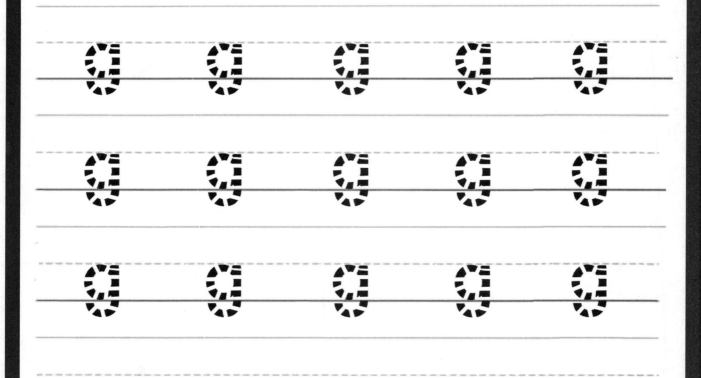

gains

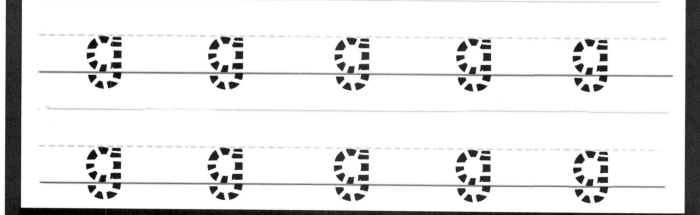

h

h h h h h

h h h h h

h h h h h

high-yield savings

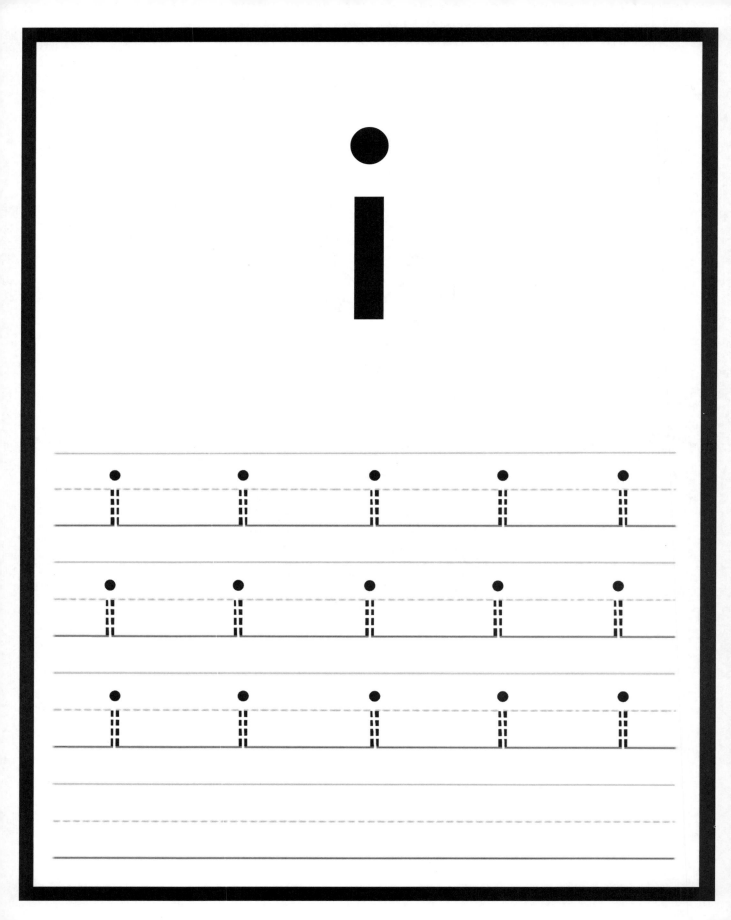

investment

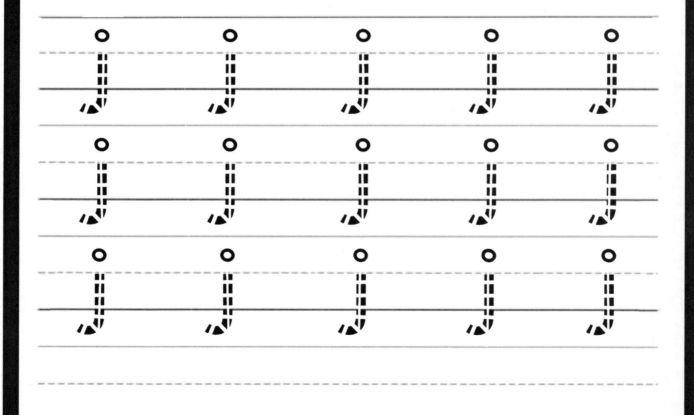

justified

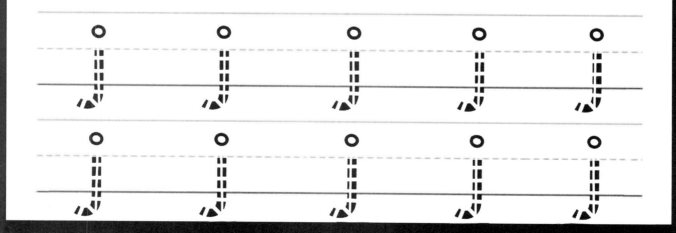

k

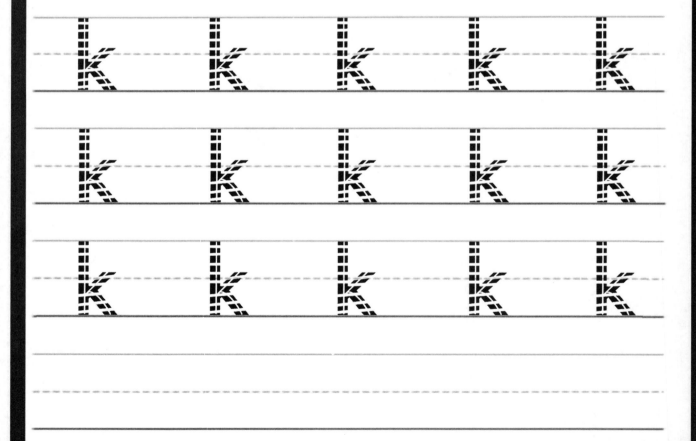

key currency

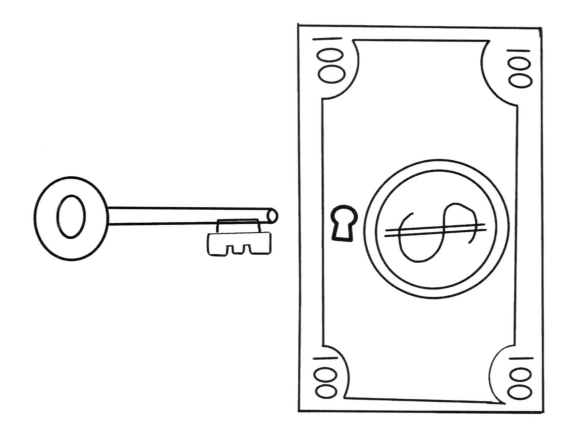

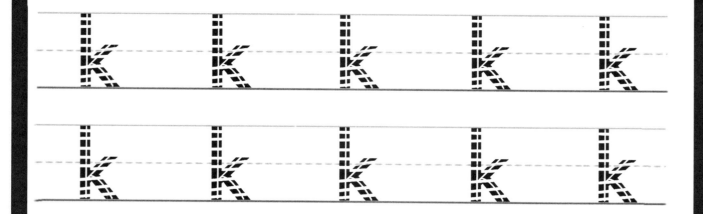

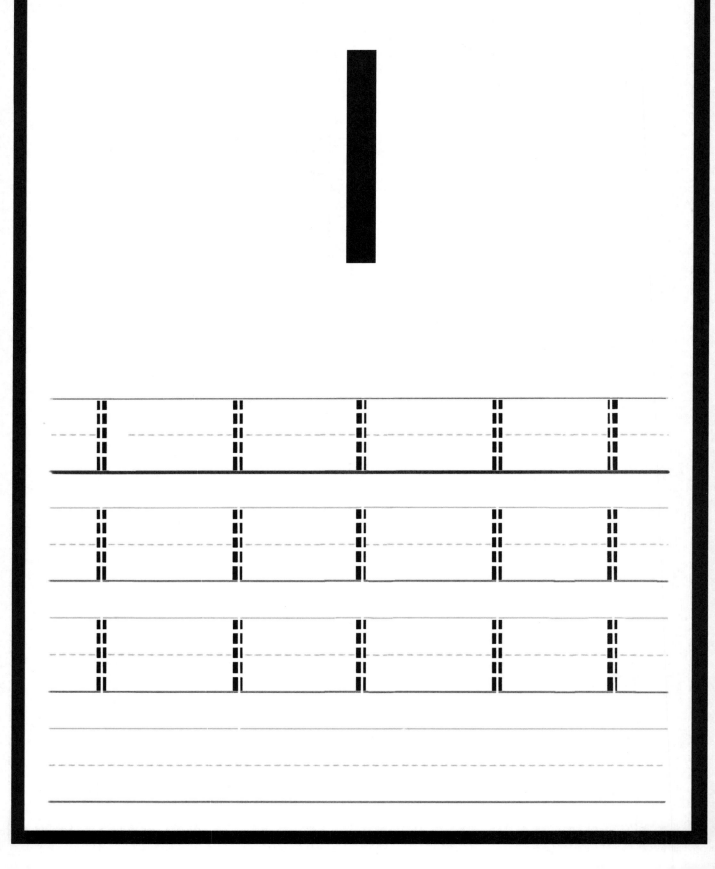

liability

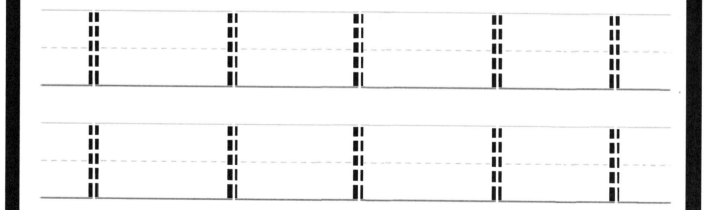

m

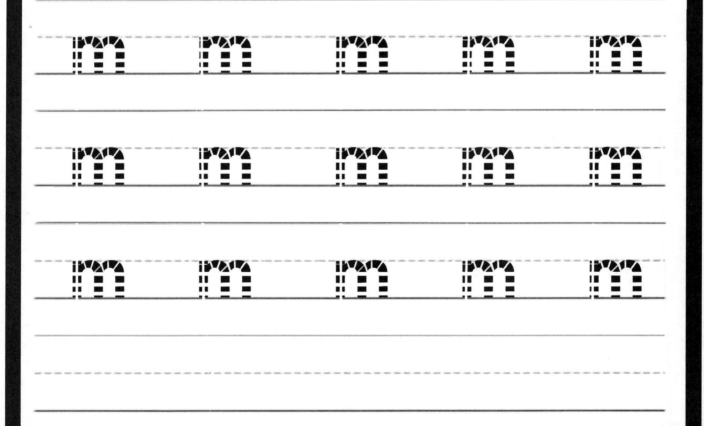

money

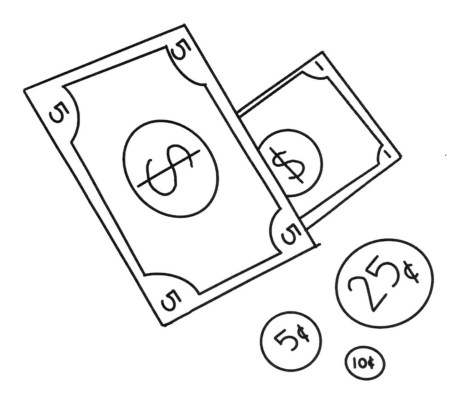

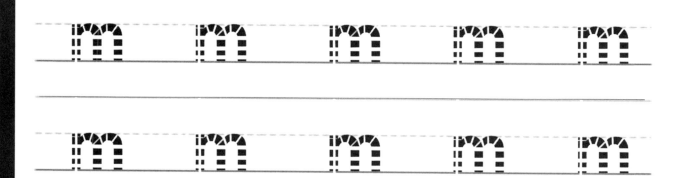

n

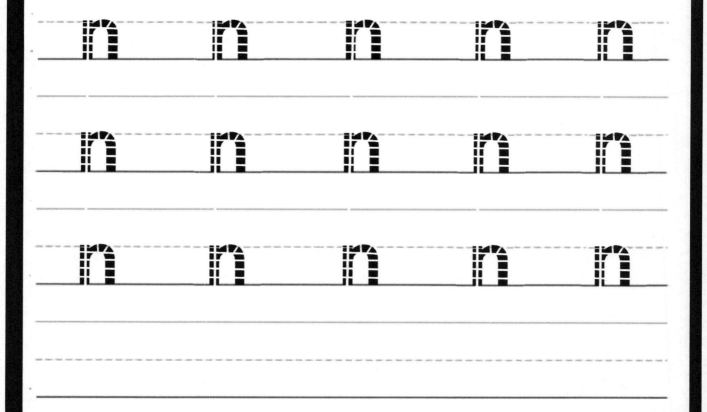

nasdaq

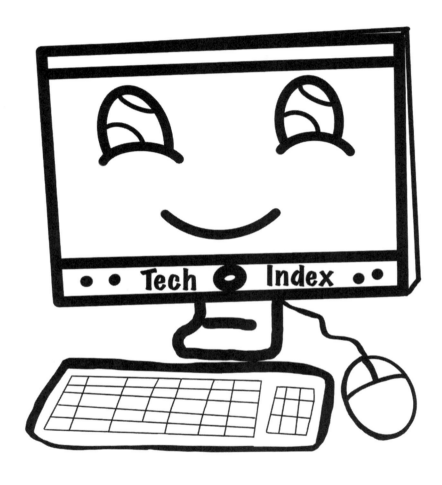

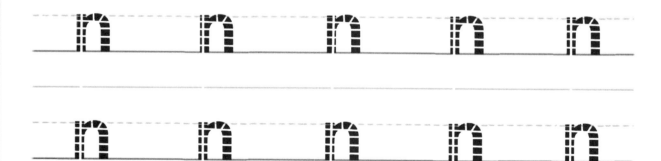

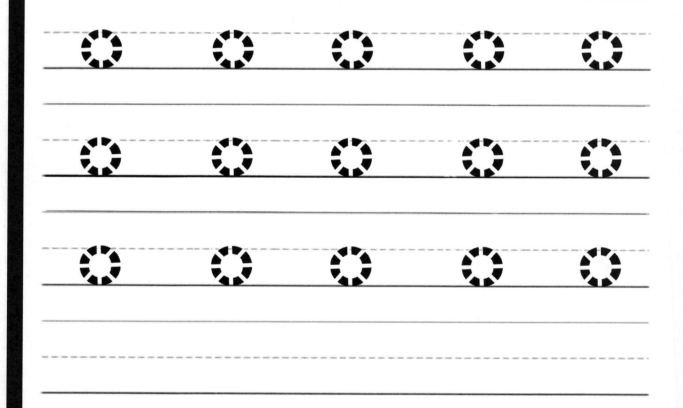

opening bell

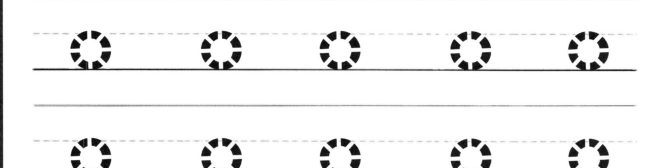

p

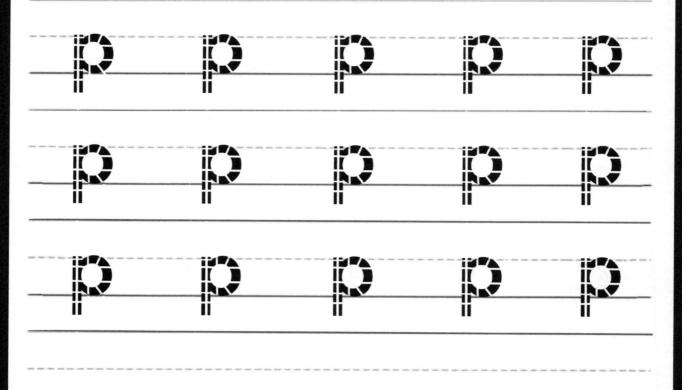

portfolio

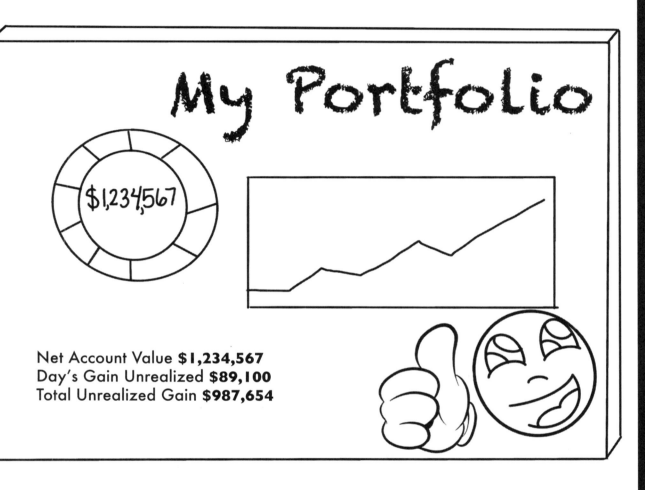

My Portfolio

$1,234,567

Net Account Value **$1,234,567**
Day's Gain Unrealized **$89,100**
Total Unrealized Gain **$987,654**

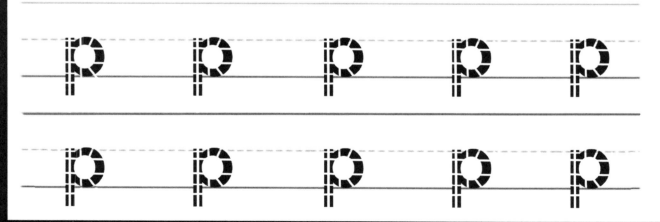

q

q q q q q

q q q q q

q q q q q

quote

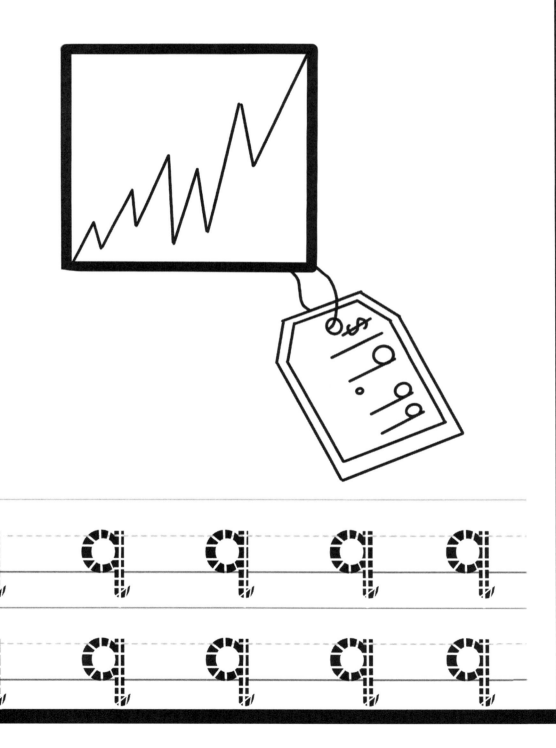

q q q q q

q q q q q

r

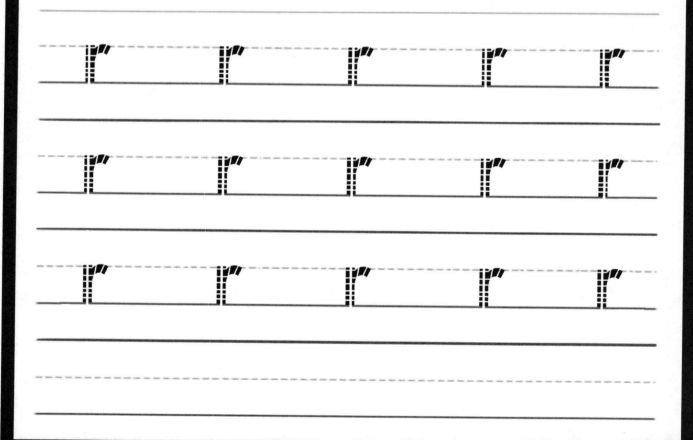

risk

S

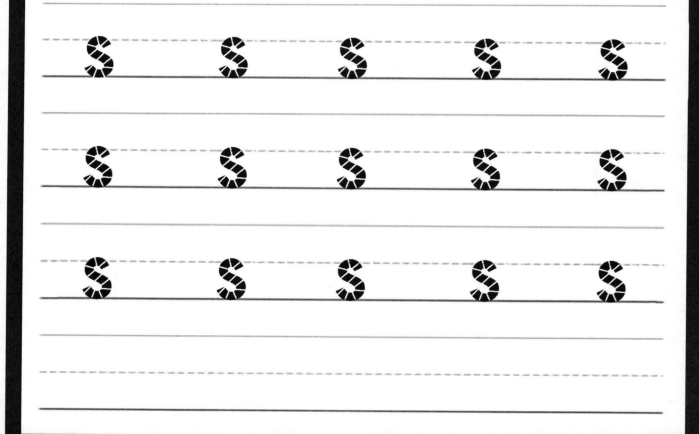

stock

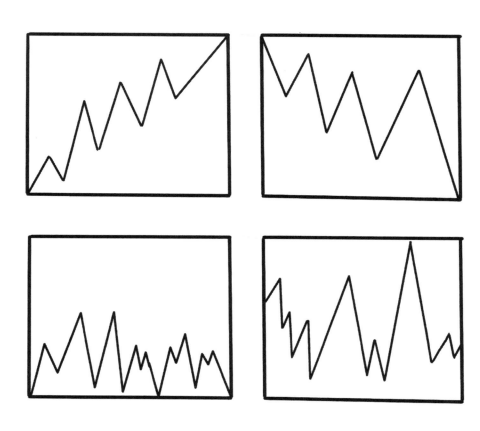

S   S   S   S   S

S   S   S   S   S

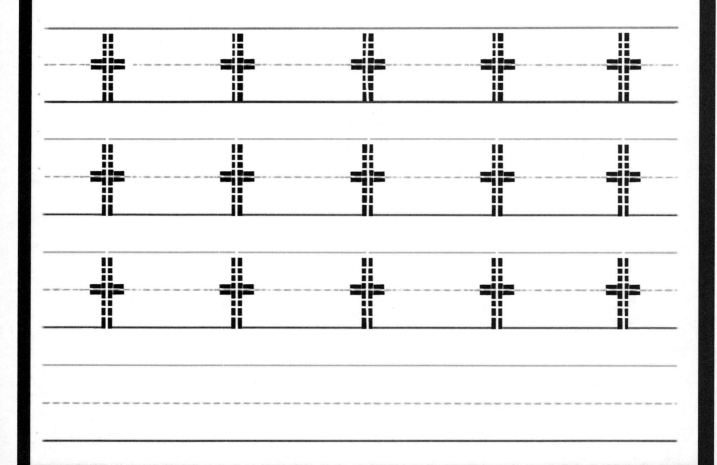

ticker symbol

TSLA

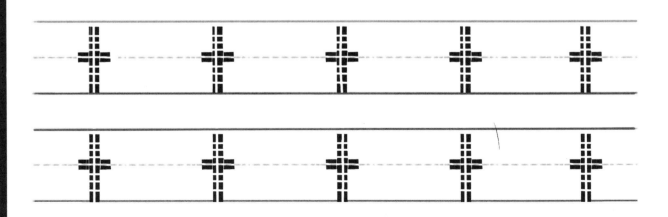

U

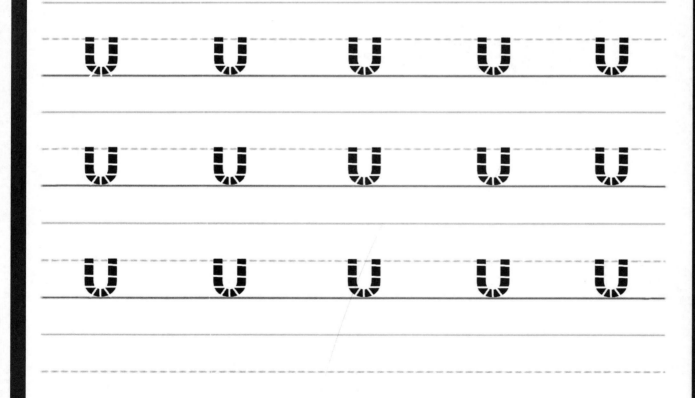

unemployment

U U U U U

U U U U U

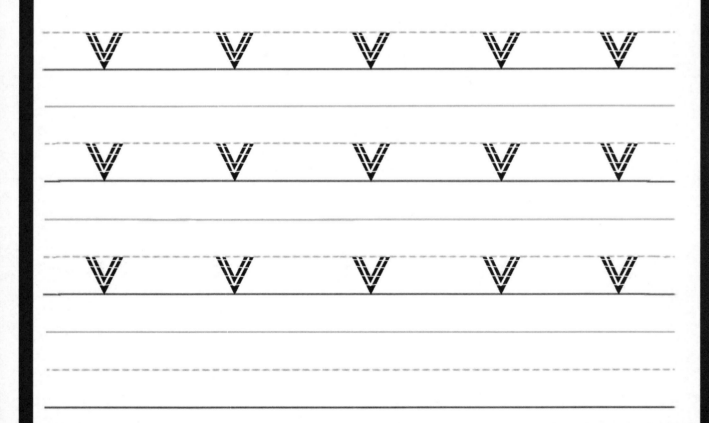

value

V V V V V

V V V V V

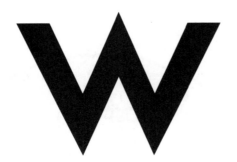

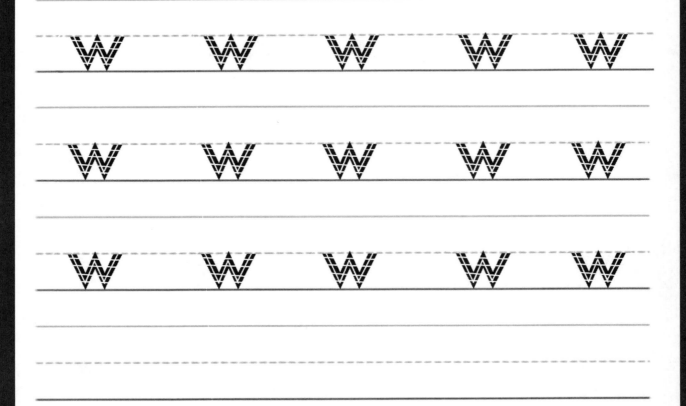

wall street

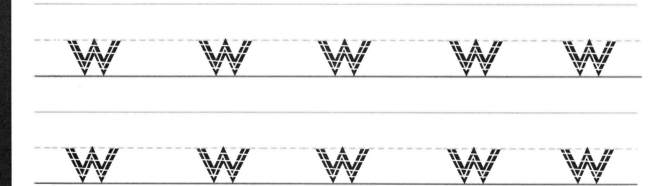

X

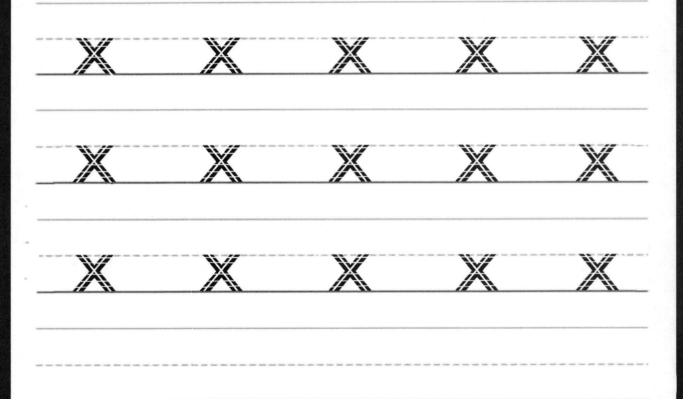

x marks the spot

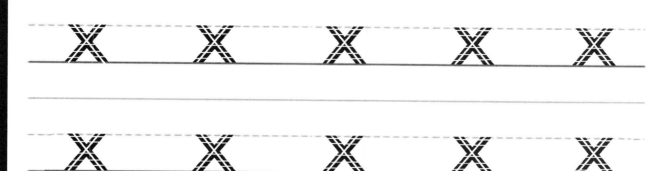

y

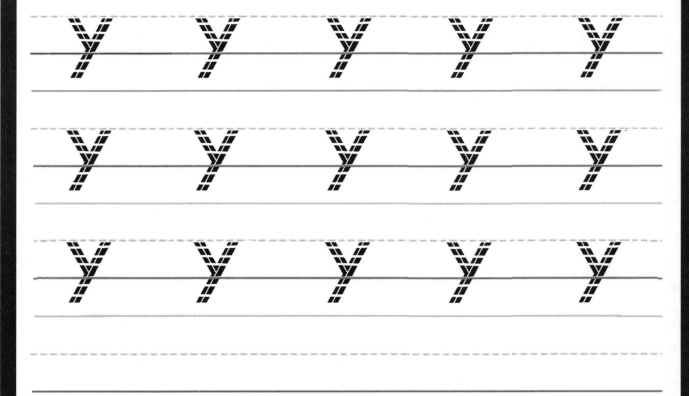

yield

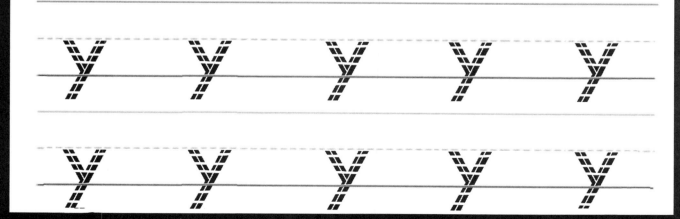

Z

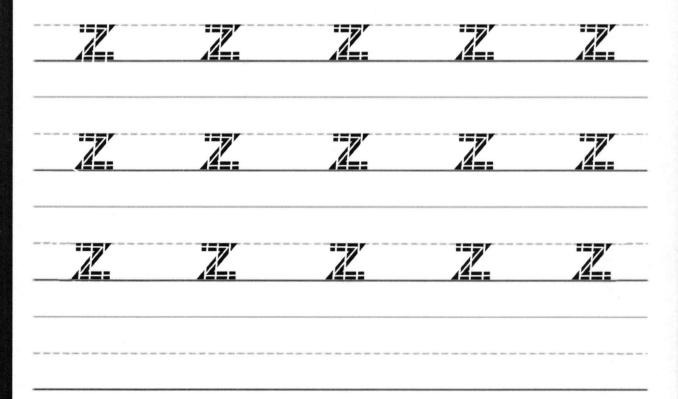

zero

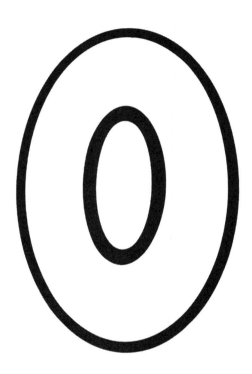

When you first open an account
you start at zero dollars.

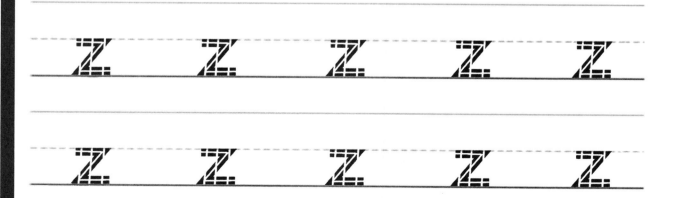

Always do research on the stocks you want to invest in.

Make sure it is a company you enjoy learning about.

A New Generation of Investors

What kind of investor will you be?

Investment Farm

Did you know queen ants can clone themselves?

They send their clones out to work, so we must do the same with our money.

Quarterly Earnings Call

Buy stocks like groceries
NOT perfume!

Dow Jones

Tracks the daily price movements
of 30 large companies.

I

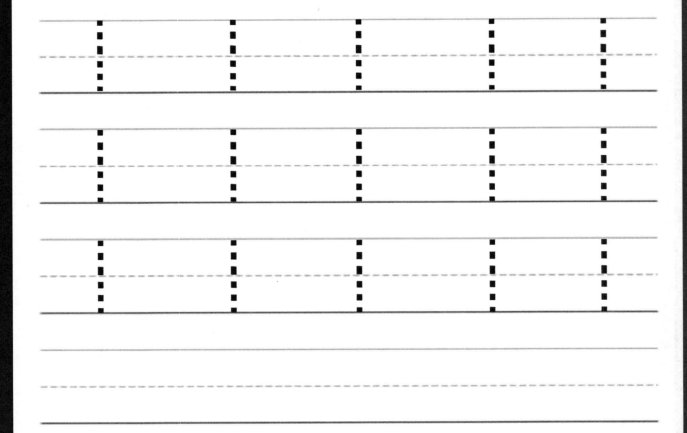

2

$ $

2 2 2 2 2

2 2 2 2 2

2 2 2 2 2

3

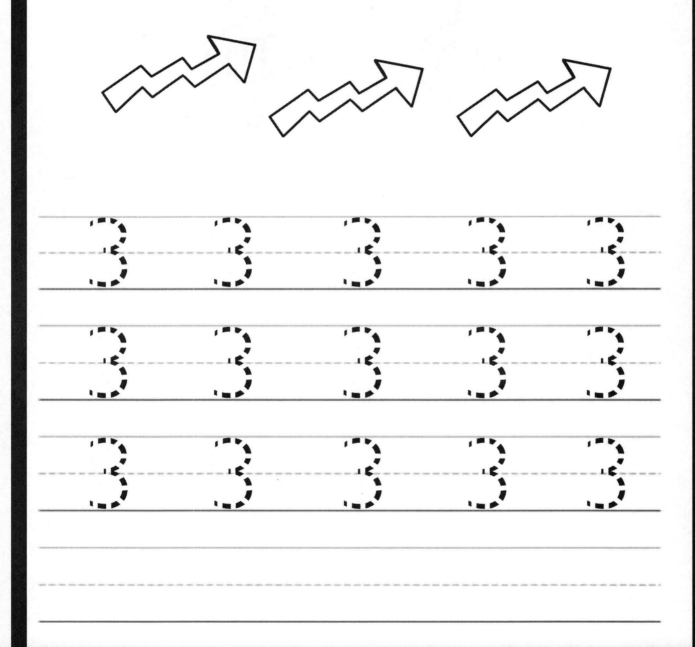

4

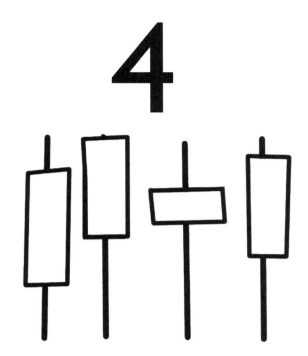

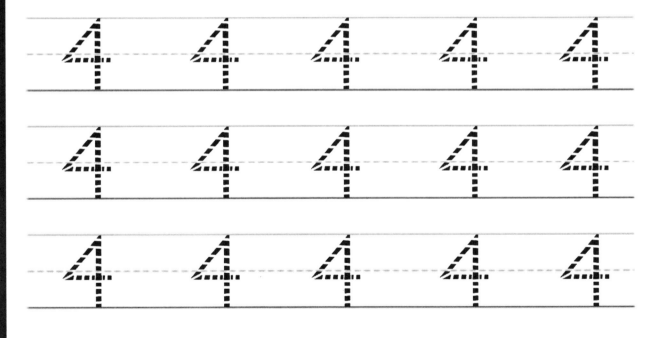

5

5 5 5 5 5

5 5 5 5 5

5 5 5 5 5

6

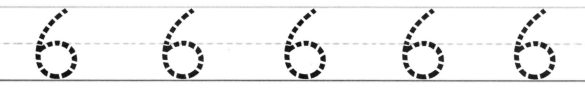

7

7 7 7 7 7

7 7 7 7 7

7 7 7 7 7

8

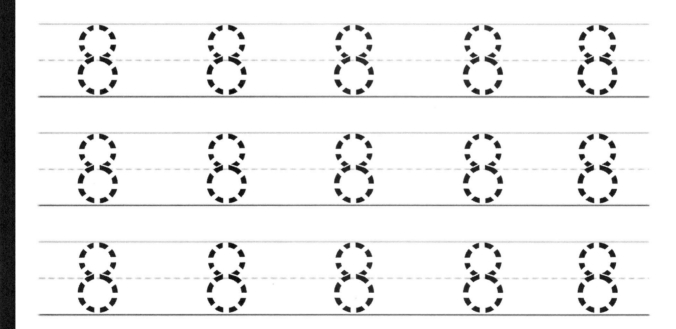

9

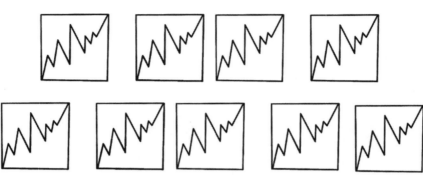

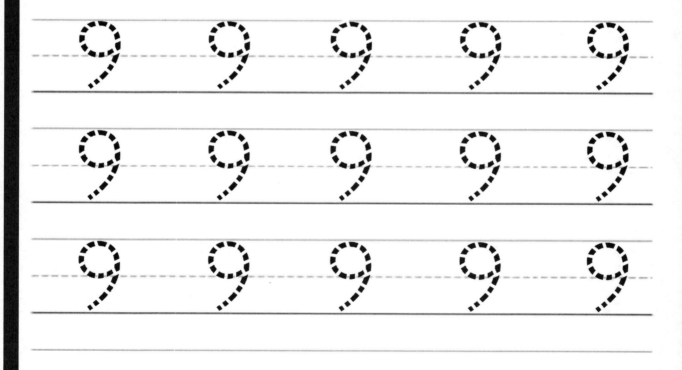

10

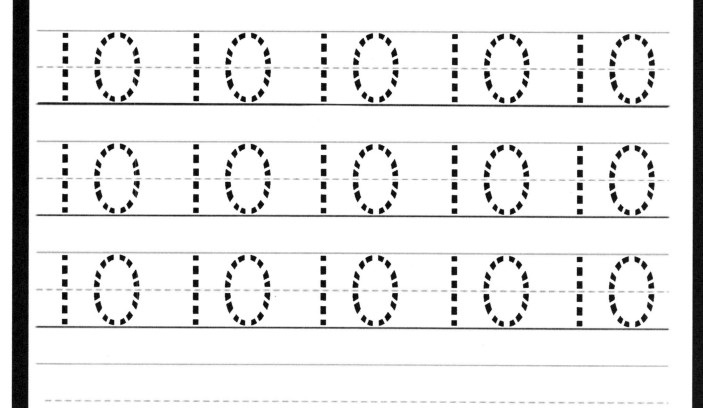

1	1	1	
2	2	2	
3	3	3	
4	4	4	
5	5	5	
6	6	6	
7	7	7	
8	8	8	
9	9	9	
10	10	10